# How to Draw Monkeys Step-by-Step Guide

Best Monkey Drawing Book for You and Your Kids

BY

# ANDY HOPPER

© 2019 Andy Hopper All Rights Reserved

# Copyright Notes

The material in question, hereto referred to as The Book, may not be reproduced in any part by any means without the explicit permission of the bearer of the material, hereto known as the Author. Reproduction of The Book includes (but is not limited to) any printed copies, electronic copies, scanned copies or photocopies.

The Book was written as an informational guide and nothing more. The Reader assumes any and all risk when following the suggestions or guidelines found therein. The Author has taken all precautions at ensuring accuracy in The Book but assumes no responsibility if any damage is caused by misinterpretation of the information contained therein.

# Table of Contents

Introduction ..................................................................... 4

How to draw monkey 1 ................................................. 5

How to draw monkey 2 ............................................... 20

How to draw monkey 3 ............................................... 38

How to draw monkey 4 ............................................... 55

How to draw monkey 5 ............................................... 71

How to draw monkey 6 ............................................... 87

How to draw monkey 7 ............................................. 105

About the Author ..................................................... 123

# Introduction

Kids have this intense desire to express themselves the ways they know how to. During their formative years, drawing all sorts is on top of their favorite things to do. You ought to encourage as it boosts their creativity and generally advances their cognitive development.

This book is written to give you and your kids the smoothest drawing experience with the different guides and instructions on how to draw different kinds of objects and animals. However, you should note that drawing, like everything worthwhile, requires a great deal of patience and consistency. Be patient with your kids as they wade through the tips and techniques in this book and put them into practice. Now, they will not get everything on the first try, but do not let this deter them. Be by their side at every step of the way and gently encourage them. In no time, they will be perfect little creators, and you, their trainer.

Besides, this is a rewarding activity to do as it presents you the opportunity of hanging out with your kids and connecting with them in ways you never knew was possible. The book contains all the help you need, now sit down with them and help them do this.

That is pretty much all about it - we should start this exciting journey now, shouldn't we?

# How to draw monkey 1

1. Draw a curved oval shape for the face.

2. Draw a rectangular head.

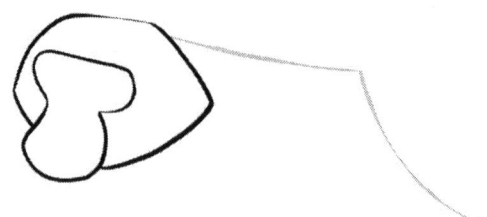

3. Draw two interconnected body lines.

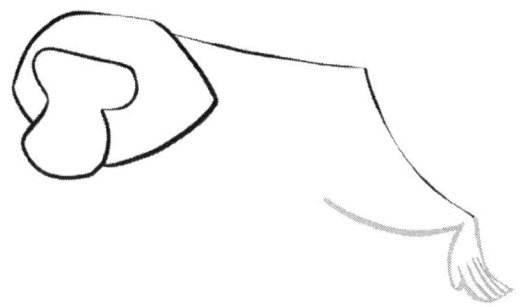

4. Draw an arc connected to an oval paw shape and finger arcs.

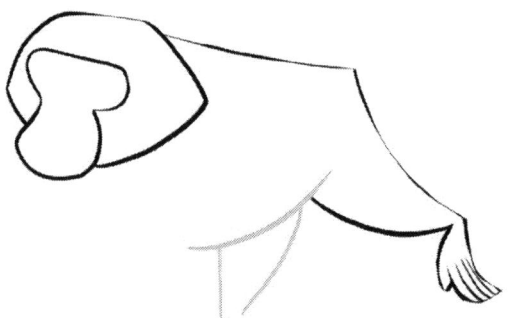

5. Draw a body arc and two paw arcs.

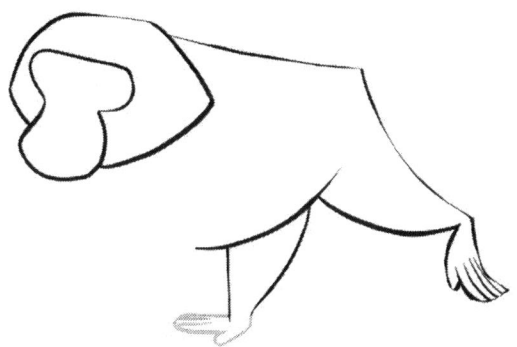

6. For the palm we draw two interconnected oval shapes and finger arches.

7. Draw 4 arcs of front feet.

8. For the palms we draw oval shapes and finger arches.

9. For the nose, draw a vertical and two horizontal arc.

For the mouth draw a line.

10. For the eyes we draw round shapes.

11. Done! Fine. Go to the color.

12. Color is light brown and orange.

13. Add light and shadow to make it bulky.

14. Color version.

# How to draw monkey 2

1. Draw an oval shape with two triangular shapes on the left.

21

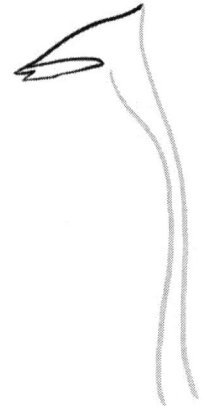

2. Draw two vertical curved lines.

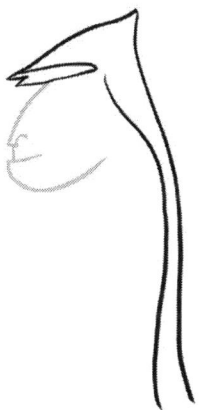

3. Draw an oval shape on the left for the face and a curved shape

for the nose. For the mouth draw a line.

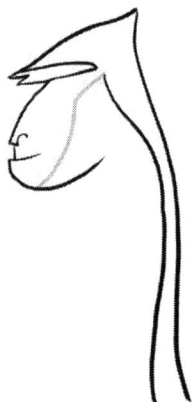

4. Draw a pattern line.

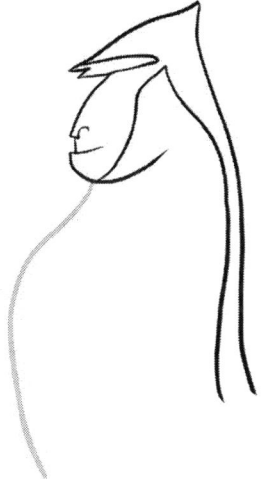

5. Draw the arc of the body.

6. Draw a rectangular paw shape.

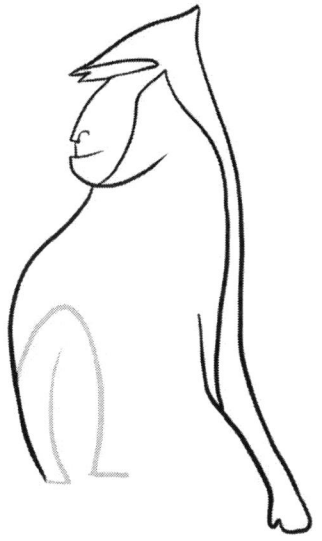

7. Add an arc and a vertical line.

8. Draw a vertical line and two curved lines.

9. For the palms we draw two oval shapes and finger arches.

10. Draw a curved line on the right.

11. Add a zigzag line in the center.

12. Draw two arcs on the left for the tail.

13. Draw the round shape of the eye.

14. Done. Fine. Go to the color.

15. Color is gray white, eyes are yellow.

16. Add light and shadow to make it bulky.

17. Color version.

# How to draw monkey 3

1. Draw a triangular shape.

2. Draw a circular shape of the ear to the left.

3. Draw an oval face shape. Add a wavy line of the nose and a straight line of the mouth.

4. Draw three triangular shapes on the left and a straight head.

5. Draw two lines of the body.

6. Add 4 hand lines.

7. Draw two rectangular shapes interconnected in the center.

8. For the palms we draw rectangular shapes and finger arches.

9. Draw two oval shapes for the legs and a line inside.

10. Below we draw the triangular shape of the paws and the arc of the fingers.

11. Draw a curved shape for the tail on the left.

12. We draw round forms for eyes.

13. Done! Fine. Go to the color.

14. Color is light brown and yellow.

15. Add light and shadow to make it bulky.

16. Color version.

# How to draw monkey 4

1. Draw the oval shape of the head.

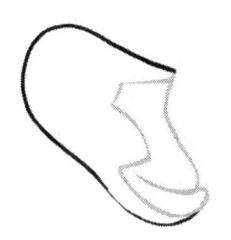

2. Draw a curved face shape and add a straight line for the mouth.

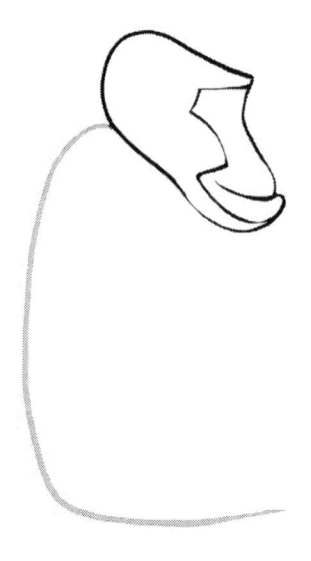

3. Draw the arc of the body.

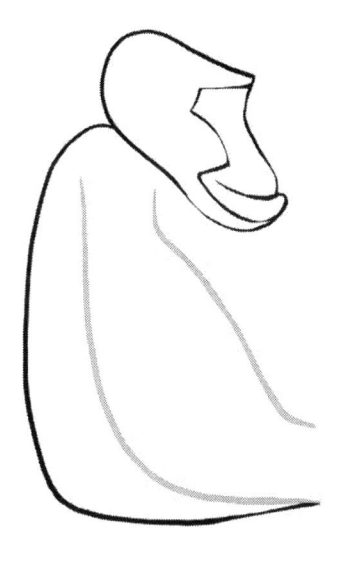

4. Draw two lines for the hand.

5. Draw an oval palm.

6. Add two arcs interconnected in the center.

7. Draw two lines of the hand.

8. Add an oval palm.

9. Draw three oval shapes of small size doy fingers.

10. Draw round nipples.

11. For the nostrils, draw an arc and draw round shapes for the eyes.

12. Done! Fine. Go to the color.

13. Color black blue.

14. Add light and shadow to make it bulky.

15. Color version.

# How to draw monkey 5

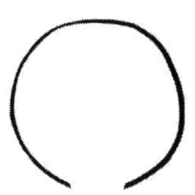

1. Draw a round face shape.

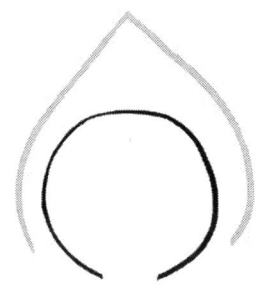

2. Draw above the triangular shape.

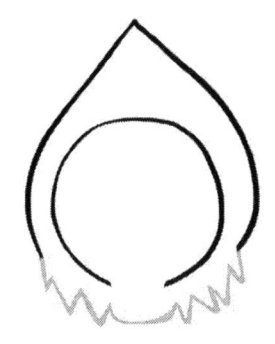

3. We draw on the sides of 4 triangular shapes

and connect them with an arc.

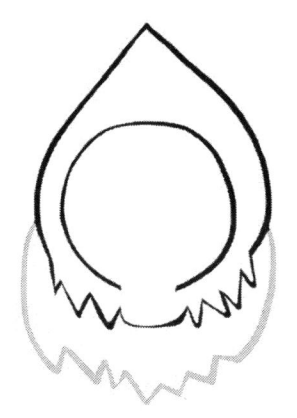

4. On the sides we add arcs and connect them with a zigzag line.

5. Draw 4 vertical lines and connect them horizontally.

6. Draw a hand to palm, two oval shapes connected together and short arches of fingers.

7. Draw two arcs connected to each other and one straight line to the right.

8. We draw an oval form of a foot and short arches of fingers.

9. We draw a round shape for the nose and inside it there are two smaller round shapes.

10. Draw an oval shape inside which we draw two lines.

11. Above we draw a rectangular shape within which the milking eye draws round shapes.

12. Done! Fine. Go to the color.

13. Color is black-gray, eyes are yellow.

14. Add light and shadow to make it bulky.

15. Color version.

# How to draw monkey 6

1. Draw an arc.

2. Draw two arcs above. On the left we draw a round ear shape.

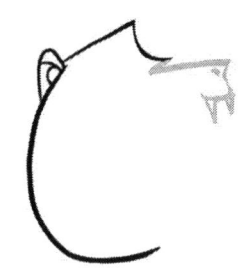

3. On the right, draw a rectangular shape below which we draw two triangular teeth.

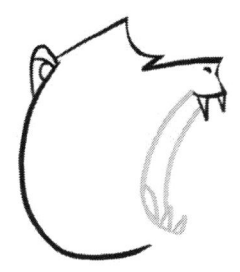

4. Below we draw two vertical lines, an arc of the tongue and two triangular teeth.

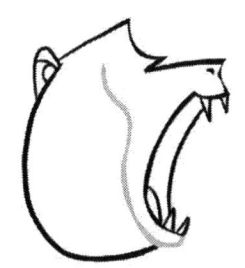

5. Draw a wavy line to the left.

6. Below we draw two arcs.

7. On the left, draw two lines of the body.

94

8. Add round palm shapes.

9. Draw the arc for the foot on the right.

96

10. For the feet, draw two interconnected oval shapes, inside of which we draw the arches of the fingers.

11. In the same way we draw the second foot. Above we draw an oval inside which we draw a line.

12. On the left, draw a rectangular tail shape.

13. For the eye we draw a round shape.

14. Done! Fine. Go to the color.

15. Color is orange and light ocher.

16. Add light and shadow to make it bulky.

17. Color version.

# How to draw monkey 7

1. Draw two interconnected oval shapes.

2. On the right we draw a long oval shape, on the left two lines.

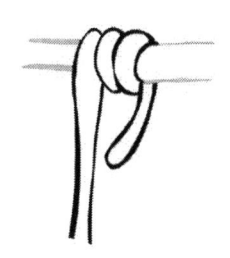

3. Add two horizontal lines to the sides.

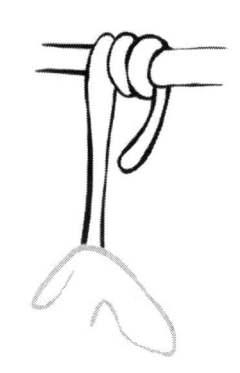

4. Draw two oval-shaped legs.

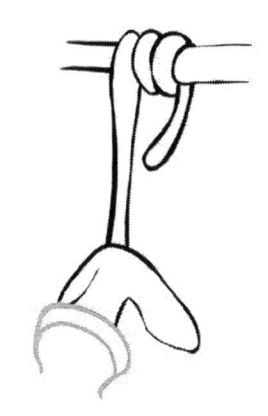

5. Draw two arcs interconnected at the ends.

110

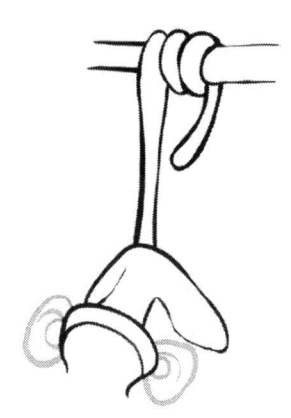

6. We draw two round ear shapes, inside of which there is a smaller barking circle and an arc.

7. Below we draw two interconnected at the ends of the arc.

8. On the right, draw the oval shape of the foot and the arc of the fingers.

9. To the left of the hand draw an oval shape and an arc of fingers. Above we draw an oval shape of a finger.

10. Draw below two interconnected rectangular shapes.

11. Draw two lines for the second hand.

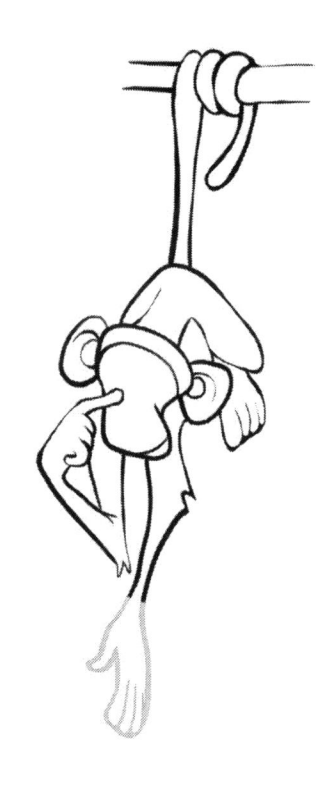

12. For the palm, draw two interconnected oval shapes and finger arcs.

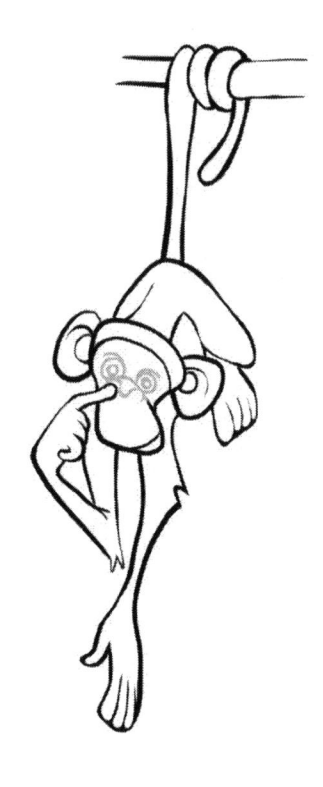

13. Doyasa draw a wavy line. For eyes we draw round shapes.

14. Done! Fine. Go to the color.

15. Color is orange-yellow.

16. Add light and shadow to make it bulky.

17. Color version.

# About the Author

Andy Hopper is an American illustrator born in sunny California just a hair's breadth from the beautiful Sierra foothills. After studying Design and Media at UCLA, Andy decided to try his hand at teaching his own unique style of art to novice artists just starting out with their craft.

He has won numerous art awards and has several publications in print and e-book to his credit. His e-books teach the beginner artist how to draw using simple techniques suitable for all ages. While Andy prefers using chalk, pencil and pastels for his own artwork, but has been known to dabble in the world of watercolour from time to time and teach this skill to his students.

Andy Hopper lives just outside of Los Angeles in Santa Monica, California with his wife of 15 years and their three children. His art studio is a welcome respite to the area and he has been known to start impromptu outdoor art sessions with the people in his neighborhood for no charge.

Printed in Great Britain
by Amazon